To my family, who inspire creativity —T.N.

To the future of all young readers —P.M.

To my dad, Angel Medina —E.M.

Farrar Straus Giroux Books for Young Readers
An imprint of Macmillan Publishing Group, LLC
120 Broadway, New York, NY 10271

Text copyright © 2021 by Mary Margaret Nienow
Pictures copyright © 2021 by Erika Medina
Color separations by Embassy Graphics
Printed in China by Hung Hing Off-set Printing Co. Ltd., Heshan City, Guangdong Province
Designed by Aram Kim
First edition, 2021
10 9 8 7 6 5 4 3 2 1
mackids.com
Library of Congress Control Number: 2020910186
ISBN 978-0-374-31399-9
Our books may be purchased in bulk for promotional, educational, or business use. Please contact
your local bookseller or the Macmillan Corporate and Premium Sales Department at (800) 221-7945
ext. 5442 or by email at MacmillanSpecialMarkets@macmillan.com.

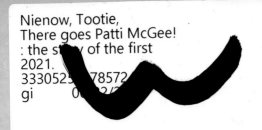
THERE GOES

Patti McGee!

THE STORY OF THE FIRST WOMEN'S NATIONAL SKATEBOARD CHAMPION

Words by

Tootie Nienow

Pictures by

Erika Medina

Farrar Straus Giroux
New York

There goes Patti McGee!

Bold!

Confident!

Courageous!

One day, a group of boys zipped past Patti's house, each riding a board with wheels. She'd *never* seen anything like it before! She had to give it a try.

Patti ripped the wheels off her roller skates and nailed them to an old board.

She stood at the top of the tallest hill
in her neighborhood.

ZIP! SWISH! ZOOM! CRASH!

She popped up and brushed herself off.

"That was so cool!" she whooped.

A group of girls nearby laughed and yelled,

"Patti, don't be such a tomboy!"

Their words hurt her a little, but Patti ran back up

the hill anyway. She wanted to try it again!

Eventually, Patti wanted something better than her old board. Her brother shaped another one for her in woodshop. On it, she could . . .

Patti carried her skateboard everywhere, always on the lookout for a bigger hill, the biggest thrill.

When people sneered, Patti smiled.
When they yelled "Get off the sidewalk,"
all she heard was the click of her board
over every crack as she glided along.

But as Patti learned more and more tricks, the wheels
on her trusty board started to fall off at every turn.

Patti had to get a new one somehow.

She admired some through the store window.
But they cost so much money!

Then she heard that George Cooley, one of the
first board builders in skateboarding, was
starting a team and giving its members
free boards.

Patti *had* to get on the team, but all the other members
were boys.

Would George's boys let a girl skate with them?

Patti decided to spy on them and practice their tricks so she could impress George.

She copied surfing moves and made them her own.

NOSE WHEEL

HANGING HEELS

THE COFFIN

Patti mastered them all.

One day, Patti grabbed her old skateboard and followed George Cooley to a demonstration. She Walked-the-Board, Nose Wheeled, and Switched Ends in front of George, hoping and hoping he would notice.

George was impressed. He invited Patti to skate on his team and gave her a free board. Patti ran her hand across the smooth deck and spun the new wheels. She couldn't wait to hop on and give it a whirl. The Cooley boys welcomed Patti to the team. "Wow, Patti, you're really good!" they said.

Patti and the Cooley boys sped around town.
New tricks were invented every day.
Patti and the boys tried them out.

KICK TURN

CATAMARAN

Patti and the boys skated past a poster. She stopped for a closer look. There was going to be a skateboard championship. "You should enter, Patti. You could definitely win," the boys said.

Patti wanted to show off her skills.

She wanted to *win*!

Patti started practicing.

She perfected the Figure 8: two perfect circles connected with one push at the intersection.

She mastered the Jump-the-Stick: rolling, jumping, and landing on the board . . .

But she couldn't figure out what to do for the freestyle section. She had to dazzle the judges with her trick.

I can choose anything, Patti thought. *Maybe a kick flip or hanging heels. Or maybe I can do something new.*

She experimented every day. Her trick had to be spectacular.

Around and around, back and forth, up and down,
and just for fun, she cartwheeled and walked handstands.

That's it! Patti thought. *Skateboarding is all about
having fun. And this trick is the* most *fun!*

Then the work began. Five hours a day!

Feet together. Toes pointed.

Crash! Crash! Crash!

It wasn't easy. Her arms ached and her knuckles bled.

On the day she balanced perfectly for six seconds, she knew she was ready.

When competition day arrived, butterflies kick flipped in Patti's stomach.

Sixty skaters practiced as they waited for their turn to compete. The girls competing were a drop among an ocean of boys.

"Welcome to the first National Skateboard Championship," the announcer said.

Patti's heart pounded in her chest.

Soon it was her turn.

"Next up, Patti McGee!" the announcer boomed.

Patti performed a perfect Figure 8.
She nailed Jump-the-Stick.

And then it was time for the freestyle event.
Now she could show everyone her secret trick.

Patti grasped her deck, ran a couple of steps, and kicked up her feet. *Feet together, toes pointed*, she thought as she glided for

four . . .

five . . .

six seconds.

It was perfect!

Patti jumped off her board and pumped her fist in the air.

Then she saw the judges' stunned faces.

Patti stood center stage, alone, her competitors to the side.

A hundred spectators eyed the judges and held their breath.

The judges looked at one another and searched their scorecards.

Time seemed to stand still.

Slowly, the judges flipped their cards . . .

A perfect score!

The crowd erupted into cheers for Patti.

She'd won!

Where Is She Now?

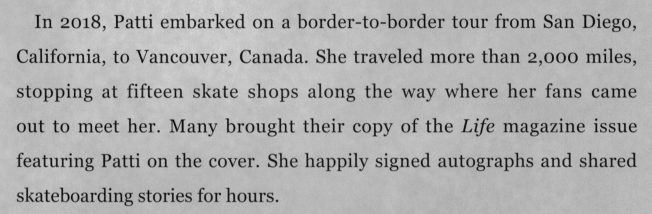

Patti McGee continues to inspire young skaters.

At the Venice Annual Ladies Skateboard Jam in Los Angeles, Patti coaches skaters as young as five years old. She loves to help them hone their skills and tells them to "skate every day."

In 2018, Patti embarked on a border-to-border tour from San Diego, California, to Vancouver, Canada. She traveled more than 2,000 miles, stopping at fifteen skate shops along the way where her fans came out to meet her. Many brought their copy of the *Life* magazine issue featuring Patti on the cover. She happily signed autographs and shared skateboarding stories for hours.

Patti is currently the ambassador for Silly Girl Skateboards, going across the country to teach skills and safety to beginning skateboarders. She even helped a troop of Girl Scouts earn the skateboard safety badge. Her motto: "Wear a helmet so you can live to skate another day."

Patti loves to pop in at skate parks, pull on her helmet and knee-pads, and roll around on her board. After a while, everyone starts doing rolling handstands—everyone except Patti. Now that she's older, she will only attempt rolling handstands in a pool or on the grass.

Wherever she goes, she shakes hands and gives hugs to everyone she meets, wanting to make people feel special and believe in their dreams, because that's how people accomplish the extraordinary . . . just like Patti did!

Author's Note

Before Patti was a skateboard champion, she was a yo-yo and kite-flying champion in her hometown of San Diego. She was on the swim and high dive team, she sailed a small boat, and she was an award-winning surfer. She was also in the award-winning roller-skate club the Rebel Rexers, which was very popular in the 1960s. It seems winning was in her blood.

Patti McGee won the first Women's National Skateboard competition in 1964. Her rolling handstand and precision Figure 8 earned her a perfect score. No one had performed a rolling handstand in a competition before, male or female. She shocked the skateboarding world with her win and proved that, in her words, "skateboarding is 100 percent as much for girls as it is for boys."

On the other hand, Patti was shocked by the size of the trophy she received. While the first-place boy received a very large trophy, Patti was awarded a very small one. The following year, twice as many girls showed up to compete in the national competition and many said the handstand was the most difficult trick of all. Only one girl attempted it in the competition and she did not score as well as Patti.

After her win, Patti became the first professional female skateboarder in history. She toured with Hobie Skateboards, demonstrating skateboard tricks to excited crowds of fans. Everywhere she went, they begged, "Do a handstand for us, Patti!"

In 1965, Patti was featured on the covers of *Life* magazine and *Skateboarder Magazine*. She also appeared on *The Tonight Show Starring Johnny Carson*, and in 2010, she was the first woman to be inducted into the Skateboarding Hall of Fame. She was so thankful to George Cooley for giving her the opportunity to skate on his team that she invited him as her date to the ceremony.

Patti's incredible trick pushed skateboarding stunts further than any of her friends could have imagined. A new breed of skaters was born, taking the sport everywhere, from downhill slaloms to empty swimming pools to concrete parks and all the way to the Olympics.

There goes Patti McGee!

Sources

Dougherty, Terri. *Girls' Skateboarding: Skating to Be the Best*. Mankato, MN: Capstone, 2008.

Huber, Todd, Skateboarding Hall of Fame. Personal interview. June 1, 2019.

Linares, Jacqueline. "Patti McGee: Her Own Skater." *OC Weekly*, March 17, 2017.

Marcus, Ben, and Lucia Griggi. *The Skateboard: The Good, the Rad, and the Gnarly*. Minneapolis: MVP Books, 2011.

May, Kirse Granat. *Golden State, Golden Youth: The California Image in Popular Culture, 1955–1966*. Chapel Hill: University of North Carolina Press, 2002.

"McGee, Patti. National Skateboard Champion." *The Mike Douglas Show*. 1965.

McGee, Patti. Personal interview. June 3, 2017, November 8, 2018, March 31, 2019.

McGee, Patti. Skateboarding Hall of Fame Induction Speech. YouTube, 2011.

Olson, Steve. "Patti McGee." *Juice Magazine*, November 1, 2017, pp. 60–63.

"Profile: Pat McGee: The Lady Is a Champ." *Skateboarder Magazine*, October 1965, pp. 10–13.

Siljeg, Sky. "A Talk with Patti McGee." Scholastic News Online, 2007.

Skateboard History Timeline by Jim Goodrich. Skatewhat.com.

Smith, Dale, Skateboard Historian. Telephone interview. June 12, 2019.